Getting It Done Without Becoming Undone

Discovering Peace and Productivity

By Dr. Jennell Whitfield Riddick

Suffolk, VA

Getting It Done Without Becoming Undone

Discovering Peace and Productivity

Copyright© 2019 Dr. Jennell Riddick

All rights reserved. This book is protected under the copyright laws of the United States of America. This book may not be copied or reprinted for commercial gain or profit. The use of short quotations or occasional page copying for personal or group study is permitted and encouraged. Permission will be granted upon request. Unless otherwise identified, Scripture quotations are from the New International Version of the Bible. Quotations from the Message Translation and the King James Version have been denoted as (MSG) and (KJV) respectively. Paraphrased scripture stories will be denoted as (DDP) to mean Dealing with Delay Paraphrase and are the creation and wording of the author. All emphases within quotations are the author's addition.

Pre-Release Edition – March 2019

Published by Final Step Publishing

P.O. Box 1447

Suffolk, VA 23439

For Worldwide Distribution

Printed in USA.

ISBN: 978-1-7337462-3-6

Library of Congress Control Number: 2019903141

This book and all other WIT INC resources are available online at

www.walkinit.com

Dedication

I dedicate this book to the most amazing parents ever! In memory of my father, Joe Ashton Whitfield Jr., and in honor of my mother Elsie Bynum Whitfield. Thank you for always encouraging me and having my back so that I could get it done! Because of your love, sacrifice, example, support, and prayers I am able to walk in it.

Acknowledgments

Thank you to my husband, Rev. Dr. Dwight Shawrod Riddick II, who consistently gets it done! Thanks for the unwavering love and support. To my son and daughter, Dwight III and Jasmine whose personalities and smiles warm my heart. To my colleagues, many of whom who are producing God-given assignments in this season as well. To my Walk In It team and supporters for embracing vision and doing all you can to help bring it to pass.

TABLE OF CONTENTS:

Introduction 7
A Special Message to You 11
CHAPTER 1:
Know your Assignment 13
CHAPTER 2:
Prioritizing with Purpose 19
CHAPTER 3:
What is Success? 25
CHAPTER 4:
The Cost of Success 33
CHAPTER 5:
Non-negotiables 39
CHAPTER 6:
The Balancing Act 47
CHAPTER 7:
Proper People Perspective 51
CHAPTER 8:
The Vocabulary of People Who Get It Done 599
CHAPTER 9:
Understanding the Times; I Need a minute 63
CHAPTER 10:
So Now What? 69

The Get It Done Declaration 75
About the Author 77

Introduction

Undone, unraveled, overwhelmed, out of sorts. These are some of the phrases ascribed to many in our society who started off on a quest to achieve a goal and somewhere along the way picked up more responsibilities than they realized. The reality check came when they were exhausted, frustrated, disconnected from family and friends, and wondering what happened. People don't choose to end up here, but over time they will, without intentional effort.

I want to help those who find themselves on the borderline between accomplishment and exhaustion and help those headed towards a totally imbalanced life get things in order before they become undone. If you find yourself here, you are not alone. We are a busy society addicted to rushing around and looking busy, even if we are not. Being busy is not an accomplishment, being impactful is the goal. Having a full calendar means little compared to living a fulfilled life. There is more to you than your schedule. Please join me on this journey that challenges the usual hustle and bustle of life and gets you walking on the path to productivity with peace of mind.

Likely, there are many things you hope to accomplish in life. The question is, what are you *called* to accomplish? How are you finishing? You want to fulfill your assignments and callings with grace, but you don't want to be frustrated, bitter, and undone by the time your assignment is completed.

Over the years, people have asked how I juggle each of my roles. They want to know how I navigate being a wife, mother, daughter, sister, aunt, friend, minister, entrepreneur, author, and more. Initially, I would sincerely reply, "His grace is sufficient." I was not trying to be "churchy" or deep. I honestly knew the Lord had given me the grace to accomplish it all. In my quiet time I was encouraged that I would not be overwhelmed or overtaken. I was reminded that I could rest, even in the midst of a busy season. I trusted that the Lord would tell me what to do as I diligently sought Him. I was confident in these affirmations and concluded that amid the multiplicity of roles and responsibilities, I would walk in it.

As you read this book, I want you to know that you don't have to embark on this journey alone. While we understand that everyone is not moving forward with us, don't assume that means you must go forward by yourself. I have found that as you are operating in your life's purpose, other like-minded people will arise. Assignment attracts allies. As you are moving forward in what you have been destined to, God-sent supporters will emerge.

When you look around at all of the problems in the world, without a doubt many of us want to do something. We are outraged by injustice and appalled by the chasms that exists between the haves and have-nots. Be mindful, however, that you don't become so overwhelmed that you end up doing nothing. Yes, our communities, workplaces, churches, schools, and families need support and action. While you may not be able to enact change in each of these areas, you can definitely help make substantial progress in any of these areas. This book is designed to help you focus in on your assignment, empower you with tools to move forward, and assist you in finding joy and peace on the journey. Yes, there is lots of work to be done, but you can get it done without becoming undone!

This book is faith-filled and realistic about the suggested principles. Let me encourage you up front to breathe and realize that it doesn't all get done in a day. Even God used six days to create the earth and rested on the seventh day. I have learned that the world doesn't end because dishes are still in my sink or clothes need to be folded and put away. Though my kids' bedtime is 8:30 pm, the truth is, sometimes we are still doing homework after that time because of meetings, practices, etc. An important key, however, is not to become down on yourself because the kids are up late, or the clothes still have not been folded. Many of us fall into this trap and waste precious time and energy. Refuse to play the "I'm not good enough game."

Recently someone was sharing her schedule woes with me. She was bothered because her husband had a peanut butter and jelly sandwich one night for dinner.

"I hear you," I encouraged her, "but consider it this way…You work full-time, you're active in ministry, have children, and a host of other responsibilities. If your husband made a peanut butter and jelly sandwich one night for dinner, it is not the end of the world."

"He didn't complain," she added, "I just felt bad."

"Have you ever thought that he didn't complain because that's not the norm?" I offered. "He knows that he doesn't have peanut butter and jelly for dinner every night. He knows that you have a full-time job and full-time mommy responsibilities. He recognizes that you not cooking dinner that one night is not at all indicative of a lack of love or laziness. You have seeds in the ground now. Each time he was provided a hot meal upon arriving home, you sewed a seed. Everything will not fall apart because of one isolated event. My point is, do what you can, when you can, but don't make your life miserable or live in unhealthy guilt because your attempt at conquering the world in one day was not fulfilled."

Organizing, meal planning, routines, and similar types of habits can help the busy person, but you don't have time or energy to join the "I'm not good enough chorus." Your mantra should be, "Today I will do my best and trust God for the rest. I will accomplish all that I can in the power of God. I will strive to fulfill the tasks set before me with excellence. I will make someone else's day better today."

My desire for each of you is that you get it done, that you accomplish everything entrusted to your hand, that you become a world changer, and never give in.

A Special Message to You

Take a moment and imagine God speaking this to you.

My Beloved,

In this season of your life you must know that I am with you. I want the very best for you. Keep pressing and pushing, even when you think that one more thing being added to your plate will make everything else crumble. Recognize that that is not how I work. I am your strength. I am your peace. I have given you everything that you need to be who I have called you to be. Trust me and know that I am with you. The enemy has come to steal, kill, and destroy, but I have come that you might have life and have it more abundantly.

It is my will that you prosper. It is my will that you have joy. Don't give in. You will not be overwhelmed or overtaken. Greater is He that is in you than He that is in the world. You will outlast trouble and hard times. Stay connected to me and stay in my presence. Don't let the constant hustle and bustle make you lose sight of who you are in Me and what I have destined for you. If you take your focus off Me for even one second you may be deceived into taking the world's definition of success. I see differently than they see.

Through Me you will have lasting results and make long term impact. When you smile through the difficulty and press through the pain, people may think that you are "putting on a face." But you know that you are being strengthened from a source that they cannot see. Trust Me.

They may say that you are being unrealistic in the pursuits you know I have placed in your heart. Don't worry, I am with you. With My hand on you and My Spirit in you, there is nothing that you can't do. My hand on you will be undeniable. Don't be afraid of the questions or criticism. I am with you now and forevermore.

I see your push. I know your desire to please Me and positively impact the lives of others. I will do it. Be available. I will do a great work through the one who is willing to walk as I direct even when they don't fully see all that is ahead. Go forward, for I am with you. If need be, I will you bring you out of obscurity. I need people who will unapologetically stand for Me.

Learn to relax. Every now and then you just need to take a moment and breathe. Yes, with all of the things on your plate, all of the responsibilities you face, all of the questions people will inquire of you, you will need My strength and wisdom. I am with you, so confidently go forward as I lead.

CHAPTER 1:

Know your Assignment

Have you heard that the quickest way from one point to another is a straight line? Running all over the place is a sure way to add time and exert more energy. The same is true with your schedule. Being "all over the place," with no definitive purpose, wastes time. You can't keep up with everyone else, mimic their purpose, or jump on the next bandwagon that looks or sounds good if you want lasting success. Lasting success commences with knowing your assignment. What are you called to do: right now, today, this month, this week, this year? What dreams and ideas keep you up at night? What needs do you see in the world that you feel compelled to address?

Know your assignment for the season. Dr. John Kenney, former Dean of the Samuel Dewitt Proctor School of Theology at Virginia Union University, admonished in a chapel service several years ago, "God is always calling us."

God won't stop speaking once you're called to a ministry. Ask yourself regularly, "What is God saying now?" This doesn't imply that what He called you to five years ago is no longer relevant, but it may be. Perhaps ten years ago you were the most innovative and patient person called to serve youth. Today, however, maybe now you have an intrinsic urge to serve the homeless or mentor single mothers. As you grow and mature, your assignment may shift.

It is incredibly frustrating to operate outside of your assignments. There is no amount of money or fame that can make up for unfulfilled purpose. If you want to become undone quickly, attempt to operate in an area you are no longer graced for. Operating outside of your purpose can lead to tremendous unfulfillment and can even develop into bitterness.

Surround yourself with people who encourage you to operate in your assignment and are not so consumed by their own agenda, that they can't help you find your assignment. It's not always easy or popular to operate in your assignment. It may not be convenient, but it is fulfilling.

It is imperative that you know what you do well. Give your all to that. It is what I call the "Chick-fil-A principle." Chick-fil-A, an incredibly successful restaurant, knows what they do well, and they have capitalized on it. They don't do everything, but they arguably have some of the best chicken anywhere. You can't get a steak or hot dog at Chick-fil-A. They put their energy and effort into chicken, and their popularity and sales reflect the benefits of that decision.

Years ago, I remember watching a television special on fast food empires. They were interviewing McDonald's owners and influencers. They presented the highs and lows in sales that McDonald's had experienced over the years. The interviewer inquired about possible culprits for the seasons of decline throughout the chain's history. One of the leaders matter-of-factly replied, "I know what happened. We took our eyes off the fries."

This may sound trivial to some, but what they grew to understand was that they could not deviate from what they did well. If fries are driving people to your restaurant, then doesn't it make sense to highlight and focus on the fries? I am encouraging you to find that thing, that calling, that gifting that draws out the best in you. This discovery may take some time, but it will be well worth it.

In order to know your assignment, you must know you. Not the edited Photoshop version of you, the real you. This self-analysis embraces strengths and acknowledges weaknesses. You need not be modest about what you are good at, nor do you need to harp on your shortcomings. We all have both. I contend that the most successful people are continually strengthening and operating in their strong suits. You are not called to everything but give your everything to your calling.

Don't be deterred from your assignment because of what others' gifts look like. We have formed ideas in our minds of which callings or assignments "look good" or are more prestigious. In the business arena we want the corner office with the personal assistant. Those symbols can signal success or one who "has arrived." In the ministerial world we want huge followings and the approval of people. If you are lured away from your calling, you will leave your assignment unfinished. If your task is left unfinished, everyone connected to your voice, your anointing, your calling, your uniqueness, will be affected. No matter how attractive someone else's gifting looks, pursue your own purpose. Your sphere of influence, and the world at large, is waiting on you to be you.

Additionally, God-given power flows when you operate in your gifting. If you try to operate outside of God's calling and gifting for your life, you may find yourself having to rely on your own strength and understanding. However, if you fulfill God's plan, you will be able to operate in God's power. It's what I call your "grace flow." It is that space where you are clearly operating beyond your own power. It is that space where God's hand is heavy upon you. The "grace flow" does not apply only to ministry, it applies to whatever you have been called to do. Whether a business owner, teacher, administrator, parent, athlete, or any other role that you make look easy. It has cost you time, money and energy, but you make it look effortless because you are in your "grace flow."

Second Peter 1:10 says, "Therefore my brothers and sisters make every effort to confirm your calling and election…" One must be careful when they read or hear this Scripture. I don't believe that this Scripture is saying that you have anything to prove to man. When God is at work, it is undeniable. Don't waste time trying to prove to others that you deserve the position or opportunity. Just be. Just be who God has called you to be and do what He has called you to do. You have everything that you need, so make every effort to do what God has set before you. Don't waste time comparing yourself to others. Sharpen your skills, exercise your gifts, prayerfully plan, and go for it.

Ability does not equate to assignment. Just because you can do something, doesn't always mean you should. Sometimes your natural abilities can provide insight into your assignment, but this is not always the case. Seek God so that you are clear on your assignment.

Check List:
1. Have you identified your assignment for the season?
2. Was it the same as last season?
3. When have you seen your "grace flow" operating in your life?

CHAPTER 2:

Prioritizing with Purpose

I emphatically encourage you to do what matters. When presented with various tasks there are some questions you should ask yourself: Is it for now? If so, says who?

You have probably discovered by now that people want what is urgent to them to be urgent to you. This is a recipe for disaster. While we certainly care about the needs of others, your friend who needs you to work for her because her massage therapist is only available next Tuesday, may not be as urgent a need as some of your other responsibilities. Everyone has an opinion on what is important, but is it really that important?

My kids do this often. Just the other day, my son bellowed out, "Daddy, I need you!"

Recognizing the tone of the voice in peril, my husband calmly responded, "Help with what?"

My son quickly replied, "My PlayStation isn't working!"

Now, to a nine-year-old this is traumatic. I am not making light of his situation, but I am calling your attention to the variety of calls for help that you get in a day. If you run to put out every fire, you will be consumed. Is it your fire to put out? Can someone else help? This is not a license to be lazy, but it is helpful for us self-proclaimed "fixers." We want everything to be right in the world, and we will spend our time, energy, and resources to make it happen. But are you called to make it happen?

If the answer is yes, then the next question is "when?" Not everything you handle in a day or a week is urgent. What's at stake if this does not happen right now? I often offer this question to mentees and others whose schedules are seemingly overwhelmed. Don't let your schedule run you. Run your schedule.

How do you run your schedule? First you must be intentional about things that you take on. It's an honor to be asked to do something or be a part of something, but the truth is, if you say yes to everything, even your blessings will seem like burdens. Next, don't plan minute by minute. Again, I am guilty of this. I used to plan literally to the minute:

- 9:00—9:45 appointment 1
- 9:45—10:45 appointment 2
- 10:45—12:00 appointment 3

I didn't leave time to transition, eat, or even to breathe. If one event ran too long, the entire schedule was completely off. This is a prime example of your schedule running you. This type of schedule, day after day, will undoubtedly leave you undone. In your scheduling, leave flex-time for that unplanned phone call, or as a buffer to that meeting that ran over.

Make free-time a priority. Think about what's important to you. Is it on your calendar? I enjoy spending time with my husband. Intentional planning should reflect that. Fun nights with the kids when I am not rushing them out of the house to the next appointment are important. Even "do nothing" time is important. Intentionally planning these moments trains your brain and your body that you do not have to be always occupied with a task. It is okay to rest.

Many of us have been so busy for so long, that we need to retrain our bodies and mind. Yes, a body in motion stays in motion, but a body that stays in motion and never stops runs the risk of losing effectiveness.

Is what's important to me important to God? Through prayer and studying the Word, we can begin the discovery process of finding out what is important to God. Based on the Word of God there are a few things that I can tell you are not favorable: Putting other things ahead of your personal relationship with God. Matthew 6:33 (KJV) implores "Seek ye first the kingdom of God, and His righteousness; and all these things shall be added unto you."

I have found that many of us spend a lifetime seeking other "things," but we forget how those other things are added. It's through intentional seeking. God must be a forethought not an after-thought. For example, spending time with God in the morning and asking Him to guide your day is a forethought. You already know that you can't do it without Him, so seek His guidance and move accordingly. The alternative is running your day based on your limited understanding and insight, and then asking God to clean-up the mess. Be proactive in your planning.

God's decisions are not based on what is going to be the most popular. Yes, He told Abraham that he would make his name great, but that is not the aim of your life. Your name is made great when you operate in obedience and make His name great. Your name is made great when you, like Jesus, humble yourself. Your name is made great when you allow God to be the core of your decision-making processes. You are headed for self-destruction when you begin to want recognition and honor.

Why? A person who yearns for the approval and honor of people becomes so consumed with other opinions that they live life based on what others say. It's what Joyce Meyer calls "approval addiction." This is dangerous because it lends itself to forgetting the reason you do what you do. Remembering the "why" drives you. The "why" keeps you going when others are not watching or patting you on the back. The "why" is crucial and keeps you grounded. People didn't give you the "why," but they can sure help you lose sight of it.

I don't know about you, but the older I get, with each new day I'm given, I just want to do what matters. What is going to make someone else's life better? What is going to help that person who believes they are forgotten know that they are not forgotten? What are you working on right now that is bigger than you? You are the answer to someone else's prayer. Seriously. Perhaps someone has been wondering if anyone sees the progress they are trying to make in life. So far, everyone only looks down on them, bringing up their past. But then, you emerge. You tell them that you see their efforts and are proud of them. What may have felt like a simple statement of encouragement to you, was a God-ordained, life-breathing, faith-restoring moment.

I want to do something that is going to outlast me. It only takes a second to look around our world and see which needs draw you. The needs that you feel called to may differ from your neighbor's but go for it. We all get the same 24 hours. What are you going to do with yours?

Often the more successful one becomes, the busier they get. Can I caution you not to be so busy that you forget about the things that really matter? Don't get so busy that you forget to seek God first. Operating on a full schedule with an empty spiritual tank is an equation for chaos. Keep the first things first, and everything else will find a place.

Check List:
1. What are the top three priorities on your plate right now?
2. Which of these is most important? How did you decide?
3. What distractions may be taking you away from the things that really matter?

CHAPTER 3:

What is Success?

When I ask, "what is success" I am not seeking the standard dictionary definition. I am asking, what is your personal definition? In my estimation, success is not about how much money you have or the size of your home. Unfortunately, many of us have not identified what success is personally, so we can't possibly know when we get there. It's like setting out on a road trip with no destination.

Everyone's definition for success is different. Without your own definition, you will stay in a spiral trying to find success. Success may bring you money. Success may bring you fame. Success may bring you a larger platform. None of these are guaranteed. You have to know what success is and looks like for you.

For me, success is a compilation of things. Success is completing an assignment. Success is meeting a goal. Success is impacting someone else's life for the better. Success is mentoring other world changers. Those are probably predictable. Let me tell you some other things about success. Success is learning from past mistakes.

Success is being able to admit what you are not good at. Success is bouncing back from hurt and pain. Perhaps you didn't anticipate those definitions. Let me elaborate.

We all make mistakes. Learning from them and moving forward is key. Perhaps in that last business venture you learned the importance of having a detailed business plan. Maybe in that last argument you learned that being right is not always more important than reconciling the relationship. Success is believing in yourself and your God-given strength to try again. Keep trying even when you don't see immediate change.

I am reminded of the children of Israel when they were told to walk around the walls of Jericho for six days. What a command! It didn't make much sense. March around the wall? Really? First, that was not something that they had been told to do before. This was a totally new strategy.

If you were presented with a new strategy for success, would you be able to accept it, or would you disregard it because it is strange or different? The Israelites marched six days and nowhere does the text denote that they saw any change. It would have made more sense if they saw chips of the wall fall off at different points of time. Circles two and three would have been easier if they had seen some movement at circle one. Similarly, you can't shut down or stop your pursuits if you don't see immediate movement. Success is a byproduct of persistence and perseverance.

Not only were the Israelites told to walk around for six days, but the only sounds noted are the trumpeting of rams' horns and shouts on the seventh day. This was another unusual directive. Were they really supposed to fulfill this directive and say nothing until the seventh day? Perhaps the people were not to talk so they wouldn't murmur and complain. A sure way to become undone on the journey is to murmur and complain. Maybe they weren't to talk so that they could stay focused. Or perhaps the quiet was so that they would not talk themselves out of what they knew they were told to do.

I have found that some of my pursuits or acts of obedience don't always make sense. I am increasingly more aware that God's ways are not our ways and His thoughts are not our thoughts. If you limit your steps to what you can understand fully, you will limit how successful you can be ultimately. Trust God. Trust the process. Don't talk yourself out of it. Sometimes you must be quiet and keep pushing, not allowing others or yourself to talk you out of what you know you have been called to do. Don't stop short. What if they stopped at circle five or six? They would have forfeited the victory and future progress.

As you read this book are there things that you are contemplating quitting? It could be that you are closer now than ever before. You may be one lap from success. Don't stop short. Not to sound cliché, but you have come too far to stop now and cut yourself short of future success.

Success is knowing that you are not an expert at all things. That is good news, because that would be so tiring! Do what you do well. My husband is a certified John Maxwell leadership coach. John Maxwell teaches a concept about strengthening your strengths. This was really interesting to me because we typically are told to strengthen our weaknesses. Strengthening our strengths allows us to become an expert at something. Out of fear, many people don't surround themselves with people who are strong in their weak areas. Don't be intimidated. Know what you bring to the table of success, and don't be afraid to partake of the beautiful spread provided by others. Again, you are not called to everything, but give your everything to your calling.

It's okay to pursue success in multiple areas. Just remain clear on your definition of success. If parental success for you includes kids being committed to a routine and being in bed at 8pm nightly, great! Stick to it. Whether it is professional success, personal success, emotional success, physical success, or some other form of success, you must believe that you can have it, and systematically work towards it.

I also believe that God will not ask you to strive for success in one area while abandoning another area of your calling. Remember the story in I Samuel 17, when David was asked by his father to take the care package to his brothers who were out at battle? Here is what I find interesting about that story. Before David left to take the package at the request of his father, he left his sheep in someone else's care. He didn't abandon the sheep to move on to the next thing. This can be tricky if we are not spiritually in tune with God. He didn't assume that the task of taking his brothers the care package was beneath him. Nor did he assume that that assignment couldn't possibly be accurate because he was already on assignment to care for the sheep.

People are often quick to criticize a direction or opportunity if it is something that they don't want to do. Surely God wouldn't ask me to do more than one thing at a time, right? Not necessarily. Who told you that? God gives you grace sufficient to do what He has called you to and what you need to do. David took the new assignment, but he didn't forget about the assignment at hand.

What does that have to do with you? Could it be that you are a parent, but God is also opening the door to start a business? Before you write the opportunity off as inherently not from God, can I encourage you to listen closely?

I remember my hesitation when I started my doctoral program. I wondered, how is this going to work? The year prior my husband started the program and I decided that it just wasn't time for me. However, when it was time for application submission the second year, I could not shake the desire. I consulted my parents, who would have to help with my two children during the 3-week summer residency. They agreed. I consulted mentors. They were encouraging. I prayed and felt a peace to start in that season of my life.

As I set out on the new academic pursuit, everything came together. My parents were fine and enjoyed having the kids during the summer days. This is not to say that they weren't tired at times. Let's be honest! They had the care of a toddler and a 6-year-old! Yet, they never complained. When I called to check on the kids, they would say a few words to me and say, "Okay mommy we are playing, we will talk to you later."

The point is, they were fine. My parents had them on a routine that included the library, stores, magic shows, ice cream stops, and more. I had worried about this new pursuit, wondering about what would happen to them, but they were having a ball.

Missing pieces align when you are operating in your purpose. I didn't abandon my parenting assignment, but I was being beckoned to complete another assignment as well. Even when I returned from the residency there was much work to be done and papers to complete. I thankfully received God's grace to get it done. Once I had finished the requirements for the day, finished homework, gave baths, and got the kids in the bed, I committed a few hours to schoolwork. Three years later, I finished. Not only did I finish well, but I loved the process, learned a tremendous amount, and would even do it again. During my academic pursuit I didn't abandon my job, my children, my husband or any of the other blessings or callings on my life. I also did not allow guilt to get me undone.

Here are some questions you can ask yourself about success as it pertains to your life. Is the task successful if I complete it, but hurt others in the process? Is the completed task worth being burnt out and miserable? Is success bigger than you?

I remember growing up in, Williamsburg, VA. Often my parents, church members, or community members would take us to hear speakers that visited the campus of William and Mary. Many great speakers came through including Cicely Tyson and a speaker that I wasn't as familiar with at the time, "Sister Soldier." As her name suggests she was very passionate and strong. One of her main points resonated with me and has stuck with me ever since. I believe it was during the question and answer portion of her presentation that someone asked if she was rich. Effortlessly she replied, "No I am not rich." Then she emphatically added, "Let me tell you why. I am not rich because my entire family is not rich. I am not rich because people in my community still struggle. I am not rich because there are so many needs around me."

At the tender age of 11 or 12 I began to get a glimpse of what success is. Here I am, decades later, really understanding what that statement meant. Her reply helps me determine my own definition of success. Success to me is not solely about what platforms I can reach, but how many people can I bring in and create platforms for. Success for me is not about how much money I can earn, but rather how I can help create streams of income for others as well. While I celebrate successes and progress along the way, I am consistently aware that as long as there are needs around me, my work is not done.

Check List:
1. What is success to you?
2. How has your definition changed?
3. In what ways have you already been successful? In what areas are you focusing to become more successful?

CHAPTER 4:

The Cost of Success

Can you handle success? Will you endure the costs? Yes, victory will cost. Everyone won't understand why you make some of the choices you make. "You get up at what time?" some may inquire. Some may scoff, "You don't prepare a home-cooked meal every night?" In this quest called life, you have to be able to move forward amid the questions, comments, and critiques of others.

I remember when the elegant and classy Michelle Obama trended sleeveless dresses. There was a lot of discussion about whether this was appropriate apparel for the First Lady of the United States. When reports of her daily schedule were leaked, including a 4:30am workout routine, some of those comments were hushed. I am not saying that we all must get up at 4:30am to exercise, though it is not a bad idea. I am suggesting that any level of success comes at a cost, sometimes a great cost. Not only did Mrs. Obama look incredible in those sleeveless dresses due in part to a disciplined diet and workout routine, but she weathered the storm of opinions and will arguably be forever noted for her elegance and style.

Will you change who you are to appease others? Will you downplay your genius to make others comfortable? Will you starve your creativity to be accepted by the masses or will you, unapologetically be you? Being you may come at a cost, but the world desperately needs individuals who will not shy away from the value of success, but will instead choose to invest in the well-being of our communities. Think about the greats in history and in our present day: Martin Luther King, Rosa Parks, Harriet Tubman. Make it personal; think of the people who have made a difference in your life. Their selfless service remains imprinted on your mind.

Success will cost you time. How do you manage your time? We all get the same 24 hours in a day. Successful people have habits or routines with their time. I have discovered that they usually get up at the same time each day. They have structure. They don't just take the day as it comes, they plan it. They often only deviate from the plan if it is absolutely necessary.

There are so many time-absorbers in life. What has been robbing your time and leaving you with nothing to show for it? Did that phone call that was supposed to be ten minutes end up being an hour? Were you on social media, not realizing how many hours had passed? Harmless things can be time consumers, so we must be mindful. Your time is valuable, and your investment of time will be an invaluable tool. Successful people have certain habits and disciplines. They don't just wake up and hope to succeed, they have intentional practices. Success is going to cost you the investment of time. Time to study and learn, time to connect with mentors and people who can pour into you.

Everyone won't understand why you do what you do. They may mistake your drive for being overly ambitious. They don't know what God has purposed in your heart, so it is easier to sit on the sideline and be a commentator.

Success takes work. We live in a time when "work" seems to be a bad word. But the truth of the matter is, work is necessary. Faith without works is dead. You will have to put forth some effort. When you see a person whom you respect or admire, please know that they did not just blink and become the leader, entrepreneur, parent, athlete, mentor, or person they are. Through intentional effort and work they have achieved their goals.

We live in a society of convenience. If we are honest, we have gotten spoiled. We have washing machines that will wash and dry our clothes in one swoop. There are refrigerators that can tell you what you are out of and order it for you. Groceries can be delivered to your front door. A robot can vacuum your floors. We don't have to talk to people we can ask Alexa, sip coffee with Siri, or gab with Google. If you are in your home and decide you want something to eat and you don't feel like going to get it, there are companies that will bring it to you. You can read a book, or have it read to you.

I appreciate these modern conveniences, but we can't apply this "have it my way, right away" mentality to everything in our lives. Our faith walk is not about what's convenient. God shouldn't have to take a number to get an appointment with us. He should not have to check with our secretaries to pencil

Him in. Some things just don't go out of style, and work is one of them.

In addition to work we need to focus. In a time when people don't stay committed to anything for long periods of time, know that focus takes intentional effort. Not being distracted by every hot or new thing takes discipline. It can be tempting to temporarily shelve your assignment or task in pursuit of a hypothetical endeavor. Stay the course. Stay in your lane. Be true to your assignment. Engage in the work of focusing in.

Focusing is an art. It's so easy to see someone operating in their assignment, making it look easy and then think to yourself, "I could do that." Sure, you could do it, but again are you called to it? Here the discipline and art of focus must kick in. You can't be lured from your assignment by the enticement of others. To take it a little further, you should not be taken off-track by the suggestion of others. Sometimes people have good intentions and say things like, "You should…" or "I could see you…." Whether their intentions are good or not, the impact could be problematic. Remember people don't always recognize or know your assignment. Recognize your assignment and focus in. Don't be moved!

Success may cost you your comfort zone or your status quo living. Success will push you. As you forge ahead into greatness, you won't be content with what everyone else is doing. Success will open your eyes to possibilities you never knew existed.

Have you ever asked God, after He called you to a particular task, "Who, me?" Yes, He is talking to you! He knows everything about you, including those things that you may not see in yourself. He sees the treasure in the earthen vessel that is you. Success may have you walking through doors that you didn't even know existed.

As you continue to go further and further, you won't necessarily have all the answers, which leads me to my next suggestion on success. Success is trusting God. I firmly believe that you cannot be obedient to God and fail. Trust God. Trust His promise. Success is doing God's will, God's way.

Many people want a general form of a success but are uncertain how to arrive at it. As we grow, we get a glimpse of the promises of God and then we try to go it our way. You can't achieve a God-size assignment without God. You can't desire His will but employ your own practices. Wanting God's will, but trying to do it your way, is like using foreign currency. You must have your frame of mind converted so that success becomes your lot.

In summary, count the cost. Going to the next level comes at a cost. I have discovered that many people want the next level of success, without the next level of discipline. We want the promotion without the new responsibilities. We want the recognition without the consistent routine. We have to count the cost. What is it worth to you? How bad do you want it? In Philippians 3:7, the Apostle Paul writes, "Whatever were gains to me I now consider loss for the sake of Christ. What is more, I consider everything a loss because of the surpassing worth of knowing Christ Jesus my Lord, for whose sake I have lost all things. I consider them garbage, that I may gain Christ." Paul is not alone in his willingness to sacrifice. Remember the poor widow who was willing to give her all. Abraham was willing to give his son in obedience. The ultimate sacrifice was God giving us Jesus.

Sure, there are costs, but please don't forget the benefits of living connected and obedient to God. Jesus promises that if you suffer with Him, you will reign with Him. We are encouraged that, "Many are the afflictions of the righteous: but the Lord delivereth him out of them all" (Psalms 34:19, KJV).

You will find that the benefits outweigh the costs as David declared, "Bless the Lord oh my soul and forget not all his benefits" (Psalms 103:2, KJV). Benefits include a peace that surpasses understanding. Connecting to Christ and following Him gives a security that He'll supply all your needs. It offers an assurance that He'll fight your battles. You can rest knowing that God takes care of His own. He'll be a friend that sticks closer than a brother. He'll give you strength in the storm. He'll be the lifter of your head. He'll restore your soul. He'll give you wisdom and understanding. He'll open doors. He'll make a way!

Check List

1. What do you think are the costs of success?
2. What are some of the practices of successful people?
3. What are the benefits that outweigh the costs?

CHAPTER 5:

Non-negotiables

If you are going to get it done without becoming undone you are going to have to have some non-negotiables: areas that you are not willing to bend on. In the pursuit of success, unfortunately, people sometimes lose sight of their core values.

First, I would suggest that your God-time be non-negotiable. As Matthew 6:33 says "Seek ye first the kingdom of God, and his righteousness; and all these things will be added…" Focusing on Someone bigger, stronger, wiser helps keep things in perspective. It makes it more difficult to get sucked into unethical and compromising behaviors.

Personal re-fill time should also be a must in your schedule and planning. It doesn't have to be anything significant that breaks the bank, but you will be better for it. Sitting and enjoying a cup of coffee, relaxing at the spa, dinner with friends, or time at the gym can give you the mental break that you need. Perhaps cuddling up with a good book, going for a walk, or watching a good movie is more your speed. I can't tell you what to do but find something that refills you so that you are not pouring from an empty place. You can't operate at a genuinely impactful level without taking time to refill.

You are made up of mind, body, and spirit, so each part of you needs to be refilled. Your brain needs to rest, your body needs to relax, your soul needs to be renewed. Each of these is important. If any of them is out of sync, other things can fall apart. For example, your mind may be relaxed, and your body may be healthy and in shape, but if your spirit is depleted or empty, you cannot operate at your best. It's hard to pour when you are empty, and as women, we pour often. Let's not begin to pour out bitterness and anger because we have voids. You can only give what you have, so for yourself and all those connected to you, keep refilling.

"Nothing planned" days can be another helpful non-negotiable. You will be surprised the toll that a never-ending to-do list has on your psyche. Conversely, there is a peace associated with having nothing planned. This doesn't mean that you don't do anything, it just means you don't have to, and you are flexible.

You may want to ask yourself, when is "enough"? Is "enough" when you have a specific dollar amount in the bank? Is "enough" when you are so tired you can't move? Successful people are flexible, but they also know how to set boundaries. They are not driven by every opportunity or invitation. They are settled and disciplined to discern the difference between a God-given calling and a possible distraction disguised as an opportunity.

Questions that can help you discern include: Is this opportunity in line with what I do or am called to do? Do I know someone that has that area of expertise? For example, if you called and asked me to speak to a group of senior citizen couples about financial investments, I would have to pause for a moment. While I love talking to groups, I know that investing is not my strong suit. I could easily refer you to my mother, however, who had a successful 40-plus year banking career. In that opportunity, I would be a better resource than a speaker pretending to know about investments. Sometimes turning down or referring an opportunity is the best way to handle an invitation.

For me, another non-negotiable is anything that is going to compromise my character. I am not willing to complete a task at the sake of losing my integrity or compromising who I am. In the moment, you may be so ambitious or hungry for something that you are willing to do whatever it takes to achieve it. I sincerely believe that the joy of completing a task is severely diminished if one has to backbite, sabotage, or harm someone or something to make it happen. The stage for success has space for us all. There are enough categories that fall under greatness that each of us can have our own entry. We should not act like success is limited—it is a horizon-less pursuit. Success is available to all of us because there is much to be done.

Consider the many areas of success in our world: politically, socially, spiritually, academically, physically, and so many more. Be great in your area of calling and celebrate other people's achievements. Help others achieve their goals. In the pursuit of success, don't step on people. We can rise together.

I would recommend you set some non-negotiables for your life. Begin like this:

No matter what, I will _____.

Or, No matter what I will not, _____.

For example: No matter what, I will stay true to who God has called me to be. No matter what, I will not harm others on my way to success. No matter what, I will press through hardships. No matter what, I will not lose my faith. No matter what, I will keep God first. No matter what, I will not let money guide all of my life decisions. These are just a few examples.

Again, maintaining integrity is so important. Respected and impactful leader, Brad Lomenick urges, "The depth of your character will determine the vertical depth and horizontal reach of your influence. The further and faster your influence extends, the deeper your foundation of character and conviction must be." He adds "Build who you are off the stage and behind the stage and beside the stage way before you start thinking about getting on the stage."

Even if it is just in their subconscious, people want to see their name in lights, or at least hear their name called. We must be careful. Vain pursuit can lead to reckless decision-making. Building character takes time and practice. The higher you go, the more likely it is that more people will be looking, observing, and probably critiquing your moves. This will not shake or move you if you have a strong foundation.

I recall Paul's reflection in Philippians where he says I don't just want the fruit, but the fruit that will remain. I want a lasting impact, is how I interpret this statement. This is also my desire. I don't just want to hit the mark on a dartboard in order to say, "Look what I did." I want to make an impact, carve out paths for others, and leave lasting results. I contend that this is accomplished by those who build who they are when no one is looking so that they can stand no matter who is watching. I majored in theatre as an undergrad student, and I can tell you that the stage-lights are hot. Those stage-lights are not problematic, however, unless you are trying to hide.

Pastor and author Christine Caine contends, "...it is better to be in anonymity and to be marked by God rather than be in the spotlight and be marked by man. The character and light of Christ in you must be stronger than the spotlight upon you so that your gift will not kill you."

Remember in the chapter on success, we noted that success could bring fame, but it doesn't always. There are people in your church or neighborhood who may sing better than some recording artists. Whether or not your name is known does not equate to success. You want God's hand on you and what you are doing. You want God to be pleased with what you are doing. You will need God's sustaining power to keep you where He takes you. Being driven by God, you will always end up at the best destination. People may open doors for you, but you don't want to live indebted or so influenced by them that you find yourself looking to them for advice instead of listening to God. Your character still matters.

How strong is your core? Doctors and physical therapists say that your core health is integral to the health of your overall body. I would say the same is true with your core values. The strength of your core will help determine the overall health of your life. Don't underestimate the power of your core. From your core flows what you will and will not do. Where you will and will not go. What you will and will not say. Be careful that ambition does not make integrity cloudy in your eyes. A strong core will help guide you and will help keep you away from potential scandals and unnecessary struggles. If you suspect that your core may not be as strong as you would like it to be, strengthen it just as you would your physical core. Exercise your core by making the right decisions. Exercise your core by surrounding yourself by other integrity-filled people who will keep you on track. Strengthen your core by studying, praying, and spending time in the presence of God.

None of us are exempt from getting off track. I contend that many people who get entangled in integrity challenges don't do so intentionally. Some of the people that I have seen fall started off with good motives. Then, something unexpected along the way happened. Perhaps it was something that their core could not handle. If you find yourself in this place, it is not too late to get back on track. All is not lost. There is still significant work to be done in the Kingdom, and we need you at your best.

As we are talking about non-negotiables, let me also encourage you to set boundaries. Boundaries are necessary as you fulfill your purpose without burning out. Set limits on your time and space. Is it okay for clients or individuals to call and text at any time? If you are accessible 24/7 people will be reaching out to you 24/7. Helping and serving people is essential, but you must be mindful of the toil it can take on your body, mind, and spirit. For example, if someone has a question, can they really call you at 6am on a Saturday morning. If an email comes in at 2am, is the sender expecting a response before 6am? Of course, there are exceptions to the rule. If you are preparing for a major presentation at work and you and your team are still putting pieces of it together at 2am, sure, that email may get an immediate response. However, if you are on vacation, it may be a good idea to let individuals know that you will not be accessible for a set amount of time. Trust me, you will be better for it.

People often don't mean to run you ragged, but they think that they are the only ones pulling at you, and the only ones who need something from you. They don't realize that you just got off the phone, had a breakfast meeting, lunch meeting, midday coffee-break meeting, and a phone meeting on your way to pick up the kids from school. For them, you have been waiting to receive their call. If you do not set boundaries, before you know it, you will be so busy solving the world's problems and putting out fires, that you will burn out. Note: If you run to put out every fire, you will burn out.

Check List:
1. What are your non-negotiables?
2. On a scale from 1-10, how strong is your core? Why did you rate yourself there?
3. What practical things will you do to strengthen your core?

CHAPTER 6:

The Balancing Act

Everything on your agenda will not get the same amount of attention all of the time. For example, some seasons of my life are filled with speaking engagements and travel. During other seasons, large portions of time are committed to my children and their activities. Yet, at other times I am entrenched in study, reading, or writing. Everything that I am called to in a season deserves time, but I have to learn that I can't give 100% of me to 100% of my responsibilities, 100% of the time.

Let's think about this. Sometimes you will have to balance your schedule in a manner that is not 50-50. In our ideal and often unrealistic minds, we want to give 50 percent of ourselves to work and 50 percent to the family. Sometimes that works, but then there may be seasons where you just got promoted and are temporarily spending extended hours at work to get acclimated. Or what about when your business has just experienced a tremendous boom? You may find yourself replying to emails and accepting calls into the midnight hours. In these seasons it may be 70-30. It's not that you aren't feeding your kids or speaking to your spouse. In this short season, the scale is uneven. Wait! Don't drop the book and panic. Seasons change. There will be seasons where you are in a groove at work, and you can make every soccer game, chaperone a field trip, and cook or pick-up your spouse's favorite dish for dinner.

Be proactive in your planning. Plan family vacations before you begin to put other dates on the calendar. If you have a child who plays a sport during a particular time of the year, it may be helpful to put game days on the calendar before you are asked to take on other responsibilities. This fits into my idea of not letting your schedule run you.

Run your schedule, don't let your schedule run you. You know that your schedule is running you if, at the end of the day, you feel like you have just spun out of a whirlwind and are trying to catch your breath. Set boundaries such as: this week I am not replying to messages after 10pm unless it's an emergency. Understand that you are always wife, mother, daughter, preacher, entrepreneur, etc., but everything is not equally split all of the time.

Not every need is urgent. People will call you, and you can quickly get swept into their schedule of craziness. Practically, you must assign your time. Dave Ramsey encourages those who are trying to get out debt to tell each dollar where to go. He suggests that if we do not do this, then at the end of the month, week, or year, we will have lots of money unaccounted for with nothing to show for it.

I would suggest that we do the same thing with our time. We must tell it where to go before we look up and discover that weeks or years have passed, and we have nothing to show for it. You probably have looked at the clock one day and wondered where the time went. Just as those hours scurried by, so can the weeks, months, and years of your life. If you have a go-with-the-flow attitude every day, you may be missing valuable opportunities to rest, work, or connect with the people important to you. If it's a rest day, let it be a rest day. Don't spend the day feeling guilty for resting. If it's a work day, focus in and work. If it is a family day, don't be consumed with your phone or other distractions that make your family feel as though time with them is a chore. I have found that having a plan is essential for day-to-day success. Plans may shift and change, but at least having a starting point from which to launch is helpful.

Think about it like a balanced meal. You shouldn't eat only sweets or carbohydrates. Likewise, be careful when you plan work activities or leisure activities. Look at everything in your calendar together. That's one reason why I like writing on a paper calendar, as well as using my phone or tablet. A practical thing you can do to help you visually see what balance looks like in your life is color coding your master calendar. Perhaps everything you do with family is written in blue. Work meetings and appointments can be in red. Ministry opportunities may be in purple. Relaxing or leisure items in green. If you look at your calendar and it is all one color, then you may need to be mindful of future planning.

Don't overbook. Often, to get more things on the calendar, we take on much more than we probably should. Overbooking throws things off balance. If you have an event from 9am – 12pm in one location and someone calls about taking a 3:00pm event that is two hours away, many of us would try to fit it in! We rationalize, saying that we will have an hour to spare. We fail to consider what if the first event doesn't begin or end on time? What if you get stuck in traffic? What type of events are these? Will you have a moment to replenish physically by getting something to eat and freshening up?

I am certainly not saying that you cannot engage successfully in more than one event per day. I am suggesting that you be mindful when planning. You want to do your best and be your best with whatever is on your plate.

At times, it may feel like a fine line between achieving your goals and becoming unbalanced. As you walk the balance beam remember to SPOT.

S-Stick to your definition of success.

P-Prioritize. Is this a priority?

O-Opt. What would happen if I opt out?

T-Timing. Is the timing right?

Check List:
1. How do you define balance?
2. What things do you have the hardest time balancing?
3. What are some signs for you that you may be out of balance?

CHAPTER 7:

Proper People Perspective

Like people, love people, but you can't be driven by people. People's opinions change so quickly. Unfortunately, some of us have made significant, life-altering decisions based on an idea that emerged from a friend having a bad day, or an overly opinionated colleague. Keep what people will say or think about you in proper perspective. You cannot be skewed by the looks, thoughts, or opinions of others.

I understand that there are different personality types and traits. Introverts are typically energized by being alone and apart from other people. Extroverts are energized by being around people. Be mindful, however, that despite your personality type, you don't need people to fuel you, stroke your ego, or co-sign your actions. Before you know it, you can find yourself making choices based on others' perspectives and opinions. This is dangerous because this can lead you to becoming a flawed photocopy of someone else's expectations, rather than the original masterpiece that God designed you to be.

Don't expect people to always understand, validate, or celebrate your assignment and decisions. For some of us, it was hard enough deciphering our own purpose, let alone trying to explain it to others. Don't expect people to always get it. You don't always get it. That's okay. Trust God and His wisdom to place in you everything that you need to be who He has called you to be. When in doubt ask the Manufacturer, not man.

It will not always make sense to some why you are not pursuing things that you used to do or things that come easily to you. Once people see you in a particular light, they may not understand why a shift took place. For example, if they are used to seeing you teach the youth, they may not understand why you are working with seniors now. Explanations are not always necessary, however operating where you are called is essential.

People won't always validate the decisions that you are making. If they don't understand, then they certainly can't be expected to validate. Maybe they don't see you doing such a task. Maybe they think someone else is better suited for it. Whatever the case, it is not up to them. It is up to the One who has called you. He who has called you is faithful. Trust His process and plan. Don't seek the stamp of approval from others. First, it may never come. Second, you can be approved by people, but not be pleasing God.

Understand and accept that opinions are just opinions. People are, for the most part, entitled to their opinions but only you can make them fact. Remember that people often don't mean any harm when they offer an opinion. However, you must recognize that their opinions are fueled from various places. Before you accept everyone's advice, you must consider where they are coming from.

For example, a person may caution you about starting a business. Perhaps they tried to start a business and it didn't materialize. They may have lost money and relationships as a result. You can certainly be informed by their perspective. However, you must not become dissuaded by their fears. Similarly, someone may have tried to go back to school while working full-time. Perhaps it didn't work for them, but that doesn't mean that it won't work for you if that is the direction you are being led.

Maybe I can put this concept a different way. Expect the opinions! Everyone has one. Expect the opinion, but you don't have to *accept* the opinions. Some are more eager to share theirs than others. I remember during the presidential race in 2016 people were chiming in from all over the world with their opinions about Hillary Clinton and Donald Trump. Oprah was asked why she hadn't chimed in to publicly voice her thoughts. Her response was interesting. She replied, "I haven't said much yet because there has been so much noise."

Her observation made so much sense. There can be so much "noise" in the world. The opinions of others, your own biases, and assumptions, the responsibilities given by others, etc. If we are not careful, we too can get caught up in the cacophony. A successful person understands that there will be noise, opinions, and distractions, but decides to focus in and move forward despite all of the opinions of others. You can't please everyone, so don't make that your aim and don't waste your time trying.

Consider the source. Who is the information coming from? There are people in my life that I intentionally and willingly glean from. These are people whom I believe have been put in my life to help me grow. I tune in very carefully as they speak. Sometimes they say things that I agree with, other times they say things that may not make sense. I trust their voice and the place that God has ordained them in my life.

As you navigate relationships, it is essential to remain teachable. Stay in a position to learn. One of the things that I often share is the danger of thinking you know it all. Quite simply, none of us knows everything. We know what we know, but we don't know what we don't know. Don't be naïve enough to think that you have arrived.

Paul said it well in Philippians 3:12 "Not that I have already obtained all this, or have already arrived at my goal, but I press on to take hold of that for which Christ Jesus took hold of me." That's where successful people identify themselves. Common attributes of the smartest and most successful people I know are humility and a consistent desire to learn and grow. They do not limit who they can learn from. Whether it is the CEO, the millennial, the single parent, the pastor of a local church, the janitor, the stay-at-home mom, or a child, they are poised to learn and experience the world through the perspective of others.

You are excited about your purpose. It's often on your mind. It fuels you day after day, it may even keep you up at night. However, you can't expect others to feel the same way. You are wired to care about certain things, others may be wired differently. Some are really concerned about youth, their academic pursuits, figuring out who they are, etc. Others are passionate about the care and concern of senior citizens. Both are important. However, both are not equally important to everyone. Don't belittle someone else for being passionate about their concerns. We can't make people as passionate about something as we are. However, we can't lose our passion because others don't share it.

It is not your job to convince others of your calling. That is not the best use of your energy. I firmly believe that when you operate in your calling, it is undeniable. Others, even those who aren't your biggest fans, can't negate the fruit or evidence of you walking in your call. Keep your passion. Be fueled by your purpose, not the approval of others.

If you are going to be successful and reach your maximum potential, you are going to have to have tough skin. You can't be distracted by the criticism of others. It can be hurtful when you are genuinely pursuing your purpose, and others speak negatively of your attempts. Don't stop. Whether their attack is derived from ignorance or malicious intent, you must move forward. The momentum that you have achieved from identifying your purpose and operating in it will fuel you far beyond what any naysayer could ever hinder.

Do not be easily offended. Offense takes energy and can be debilitating. This is not to say that people won't sometimes mistreat you. Unfortunately, in this world, you must choose to move forward. When you get a promotion, someone may say that you are not qualified. When you receive an award, someone may suggest that there was a more worthy recipient. When you make a decision, others may respond that they would have chosen differently. Be aware of the, "If I were you..." critics. They are not you, and you have to make choices and the decisions that are best for you. Choose to not allow the offense to sow seeds of doubt and make you second guess every choice and decision you make. If you didn't deserve the promotion or award, thank God for a favor and keep it moving. If they would have chosen differently, thank them for their opinion but don't feel the need to justify, keep progressing. Strive not to internalize negative feelings offered by others or assumed by yourself.

While everyone is not necessarily in your corner, realize that not everyone is against you. No, everyone will not celebrate when something good happens for you. However, you cannot adopt the "me against the world" mentality. Everyone is not out to get you. Everyone is not secretly plotting your downfall. Possessing this mentality will have you living in a bubble, paranoid and paralyzed. It will have you operating from a place of fear rather than a place of faith. Ask God to reveal your allies, those people who are destined to walk with you.

Check List:

1. Are you overly concerned with other people's criticism? How can you work on improving that?
2. Who in your life are you intentionally learning from and allowing to speak into your life?

3. What is your strategy for when people critique you? (i.e., consider the source, expect the opinion but don't accept the opinion, etc.)

CHAPTER 8:

The Vocabulary of People Who Get It Done

People who get it done have essential words and phrases in their vocabulary that lend to optimal success. Those words include *no, let me get back with you, I don't know,* and *I'll try that.* These are not trite phrases meant to sound busy or essential. These are real phrases. A wise woman who has mentored several people offers phrases affectionately referred to as "Juanita-isms." One of my favorites is, "No is a complete sentence." I agree and would add that no doesn't have to be followed by an explanation. How many times do we find ourselves attempting to justify why we can't do something or attend an event? We say things like, "Sorry I can't come; my son has a soccer tournament." We think that lets us off the hook easier. But the reality is, just because your calendar is clear does not mean that you should or have to take the engagement. "No" is a complete sentence.

Saying no takes faith. What if they don't call me again? What other opportunities could that have led to? Stay connected to God, seeking Him for each new step. If He is opening the door, you will know. Don't make decisions out of fear; make decisions out of faith. Pray, "God, I trust that if I feel led to say no to this opportunity, You will provide another opportunity at the appointed time."

Saying no takes discipline in a world that has an unspoken competition to see who is the busiest. Being busy is not an accomplishment. In my opinion, the most successful people are not necessarily the busiest. They have learned to master their schedules at the leading of the Master. They are not always out of breath trying to catch the next big thing, they are poised to do the next impactful thing.

Saying no takes focus. We have to be clear on what we are called to and can say no to the things on the periphery. If it does not align with the assignments of the season, perhaps you should shelve it for a different time. For example, a wonderfully seasoned preacher was sharing with some younger women in ministry. She told them that in this season of her life, she mainly feels called to settings where she can pour into young women in ministry in a mentoring capacity. Therefore, she does not accept every opportunity, or each women's conference invitation, because she knows where her heart and calling lies in this season. Please understand, I am not suggesting that you only do one type of thing at a time. I am suggesting, however, intentionality in your pursuits. You don't have to do everything.

"I don't know" is a phrase that you can welcome in your vocabulary. Nobody knows everything. Don't be afraid to admit that. Don't allow people to make you feel inferior for not knowing. Reasonable responses include: "I don't know, let me research that." You could also say, "I don't know, but let me direct you to someone who may be able to better help you with that." If you are going to get it done without becoming undone, you must lay down the "savior complex." There is one Savior of the world. His name is Jesus. You may be called to help others, but you are not the Savior. Redirecting to someone else does not make you weak or incompetent. It actually demonstrates your strength and intelligence.

Don't waste your energy trying to pretend. Pretending takes time and energy, with little to no real results. Think about it. When my daughter plays dress up as a princess and has "make-believe" tea, after the event, there is nothing to show for it. It was fun at the moment, but she is still hungry. She is not a member of the royal family because of her playtime routine. Pretending to be something you are not destined to be will leave you empty and unfulfilled. That is valuable time that could be used to master your assignment and strengthen your God-ordained pursuits. Real work yields real results.

"I'll get back with you on that" can save you some stressful moments. Be careful about making decisions too quickly. Don't feel pressured to make an immediate decision even if the person who asks is acting as if this is the most important decision ever. Not everything is urgent. Give yourself time to think through options. If you are unusually tired, frustrated, discouraged, or experiencing any type of intense emotion, don't make a decision at that moment. You may need to sleep on some things or just take a moment to contemplate. You will thank yourself later.

"I'll try that" is a phrase that can lead you to unknown success. People who get it done are not afraid of trying new things. They recognize that taking risks takes you outside of your comfort zone and makes you rely on a strength more massive than your own. Trust God. Even though it may not make sense to you, don't be afraid to try at the leading of the Holy Spirit.

Check List:
1. Are any of these words or phrases in your current vocabulary?
2. What words or phrases can be added to this list?
3. What are some things that may be causing you to struggle with phrases such as *no,* and *I'll get back with you*?

CHAPTER 9:

Understanding the Times; I Need a Minute

If you are going to get it done without becoming undone, you must understand the times and seasons. Seasons shift, and your focus must also. Know when to press and know when to rest. As I am writing this chapter, it is an early Saturday morning. My children, who I thought would sleep in, are already awake. I definitely do not want to get up and start doing things, because we all know that once the day starts, it's on. I contemplate. I say, "I will lay here until 8am. Then I will wake up and wash clothes and write." Oh, happy day!

But seriously, today is one of those press days. I have a deadline with the book, a full week, and today is a great day to get some much-needed work done. If the superwoman syndrome kicks in, I may even try to organize my closet today. I'm not making promises, but I have to get it in where I can fit it in. I have been putting the closet off forever, and the reality is, at this point, it is slowing me down in the morning because everything is everywhere. So, I press.

Last night, I committed to two days this month where I will rest. The kids are out of school so there will be no homework or practices and I will merely relax. Do not wait until you are too deliriously tired to rest. It takes longer to recuperate when your break is overdue. Listen to the signs of your mind, body, and the people who know you best. Below are just a few signs that you need a break. You know you need a minute when…

1. If you hear your name called one more time, you will scream. This may sound comedic, but if you have been there, you know how real this frustration can be. This irritation comes from feeling overwhelmed. Maybe you have been pouring out, helping others, meeting deadlines, etc., for so long that you haven't taken a moment to breathe.
2. The ring of your phone irritates you. Once again you feel depleted and lament that if you answer the phone someone else will be making another demand of your time or adding another thing to your to-do list.
3. You can't think or answer questions in complete sentences. If you find yourself here, you are exhausted. Your body is telling you that you are tired. Listen to your body. Take a minute. Take a nap. Go on vacation. Do whatever is needed to get your mind and body in healthy alignment to fulfill your purpose.
4. You are angry and grumpy at the slightest things. Your emotional tank is empty if you find yourself here. Your emotions are screaming "Overload, overload!" It's not that you are a mean or difficult person, it could be that you are just tired and need a minute. Don't feel bad, you can curtail this reaction by taking a break to re-evaluate your priorities.
5. People tell you that you look exhausted. Not everyone is wrong. Sure, there times when people only seem to

be too preoccupied with your life and are prying for information. However, when your inner circle is saying you look tired or they're asking if you are okay, you may want to pause for a moment. Sometimes the physical signs of exhaustion can be overlooked by the hurried individual, but others who care can see the tell-tale signs.

6. Assignments that used to be done with ease are now done with difficulty or dread. Maybe checking the mail with the brief walk to the mailbox feels like torture. Or maybe the run to the grocery store feels like an uphill voyage. In these circumstances, you are experiencing signs of fatigue.
7. You feel frustrated with the people around you for not doing as much as you. Comparison is often a barrier to overall success. This symptom is not as much about the other person, as it is about you. You are at the point of exhaustion that you either want to utilize their wasted time or you subconsciously lament that they are not part of this rat race with you. Don't be angry. Redirect that energy and take control of your schedule.
8. There is no joy in your journey. Every trip should not be a burden. There should be some joy and fulfillment on your journey. Every day will not be perfect. But every day does not have to be drudgery. If you have lost your joy on the journey, please take a moment to re-evaluate. re-focus, re-position, re-prioritize. Do not be deceived, this does not have to be the norm. Successful people can also be happy people.

9. You don't care about the outcome or impact, just completion of your assignment. When the end result is the only goal or fuel, this can be dangerous. If this is the case, you may find yourself hurting people, breaking relationships, compromising your core, and a host of other potentially harmful behaviors.
10. You forget why you're doing what you're doing. I want to go back to this because you must not forget why you do what you do. This is your fuel. If you forget, your necessary drive and passion will be lost. "Why" is the fuel needed to propel you forward. For example, you may not love going to work every day, but you love having food to eat and money to pay your bills, so you get up and go to work. Your "why" has to remain at the forefront of your mind. When times become challenging or difficult, that is what will keep you moving.

When discerning the times, it can be helpful to know what to do and when to delegate. Just as you are assigned to your purpose, people are assigned to you. Let them help. Honor them and their gifts. Don't take advantage of them but allow them to fulfill their assignments as well. Don't get in their way. This was admittedly hard for me until I realized how interconnected we are. None of us is the best at everything. That truth may initiate a reality check for some.

Another part of knowing the season is being honest about where you are. Every season will not be super. We all know that there are seasons where you may feel like you are in a whirlwind but be careful that you don't make a temporary pace your permanent pace. Sure, there are moments where you will pull from the deep recesses of your energy pool to sustain you for a season but resist the temptation to run on crazy for extended periods of time. Again, be intentional.

A mentor friend reminded me of this when I completed my doctoral work. She encouraged me not to jump to the next thing immediately. She cautioned that she knew me and knew my addiction to a full schedule and lots of activity. "That doesn't always have to be your pace," she noted. If you know you are coming out of a busy season, plan some rest time.

I also think that it is important to note that things will be different when you take on new assignments or enter new territory. Different is not bad. Too often we assume that different is inherently problematic but that is simply not true. "Different is just different."

My husband really helped me understand this concept. We are both ambitious and operate in our faith. In over 12 years of marriage, I have discovered that we usually want the same things, but we go about it differently. For example, I may carve out larger chunks of time throughout a day to spend with God. My husband may spend shorter periods of time more frequently. Neither is wrong. At the end of the day, we have both spent time in the presence of God. In life, we have to be careful not to assume that everybody else is doing it wrong because it is different than how we would do it. As you move into new territory, time restraints may shift and perspectives may change because you have been made aware of new things. We should be learning every day. Expect your perspectives to change as you grow and mature and see life from a different vantage point.

When you were young, perhaps you thought that adults just didn't want you to have any fun. You may have assumed that they were out of the loop and removed from the reality of the day. However, as you matured and grew, not just in years but in life experiences, you may have even adopted some of the seemingly antiquated beliefs. You may find yourself quoting people who you, at one time, didn't understand.

It's interesting to me how people who have never led anything, have so many leadership ideas. "If I were in charge, I'd…" I am not saying that they are inherently wrong, but I am saying that they are looking from a different vantage point. Someone who has served in leadership better understands the delicate dance between getting the job done and people management. They recognize the need to wait or pursue when necessary. You will become undone if you keep the same perspectives in a different place. It's good to grow and let your perspectives and outlook grow with you.

Check List:
1. How do you know when you need a break?
2. When looking at your calendar, is every season equally busy?
3. What are some things you can do to refuel yourself when you need a break? (i.e., walk, journal, coffee break, etc.)

CHAPTER 10:

So Now What?

Now, you can begin to prioritize. Now, you can start to move forward with intentionality, making the most of each moment. A fulfilled life that allows you to find joy on the journey is at stake. Other people's lives and well-being are at stake.

Hurry up and wait, I encourage. I know that this seems oxymoronic, but it is true. Rushing takes up valuable time. You get more done when you slow down, and your brain is sharper, and your mood is better. Think about the last time you lost your keys or glasses. They were right there in front of you, but the hurried place hindered your ability to see.

Now what? Perhaps you need to rearrange your schedule so that you can get some rest. You cannot afford not to rest. Your mind needs it, your body needs it, your spirit needs it. You will become undone if you are running nonstop. The only things that should be nonstop are flights and your prayer life. We are finite beings; we need to be refilled and refueled. Rest and sleep are not luxuries. They are necessities to move forward successfully.

Rest gives your body and brain a chance to relax and recharge. Like a muscle, your mind needs to take a break after focusing on a task for an extended period. You may not "strain" your brain as you would a muscle, but after some time, you may find that you're unable to concentrate. Additionally, beneficial chemicals are released when you rest.

Our culture has bought into this ideal of being "hurried." I remember when my husband and I were on vacation in Italy. We were part of a tour group and were eager to check this exciting endeavor off our travel to-do list. We journeyed with a group of about 18 other people: several couples and one family. During one of our first group dinner nights, everyone was sharing about their travel plans and past trips. We observed one glaring difference in our conversation. My husband and I were one of the only couples from the United States. We were the only couple endeavoring to make this trip in eight days. Everyone else was taking 14 days or more. It was during this meal that the vacation practices of other countries were explained to us. We were informed about mandatory time away, paid vacation, and the like. Wow, it was clear that everyone else knew something that we didn't or didn't care to employ.

We cannot overlook the obvious. Productivity increases when an individual is rested. You can focus and ponder more easily. I also discovered while doing a little research on the brain that we interact more effectively with people when we are rested. So, if not for yourself, then for those around you, get some rest.

Now what? Now I encourage you that forward is the only option. Going forward on a good day is not too trying or difficult. When our bodies are feeling well, looking good, children are behaving, spouse is supporting, bills being paid, friends are consistent, coworkers' are kind, we can move forward with ease. We don't have a problem walking in what God has for us when things are perfect, but that's not always the reality. Sometimes life can be challenging. Like when there is little to no money in the bank, you are rejected from a social circle, or the relationship you thought would always be there is no more. There are those types of moments.

I am reminded of Mary in John chapter 20. She has just witnessed her greatest nightmare turned reality. Jesus has been crucified, and she had a front-row seat at the brutal execution, her tears falling alongside His shed blood in a production she didn't want to be cast in. The crucified Jesus has been taken off the cross. Joseph of Arimathea, a respected member of the council, thought to be in an office of public trust, is granted permission to take down the body of Jesus, but only after Pilate directs the centurion officer to make sure that Jesus is really dead. Joseph of Arimathea wraps the body in linen. The body is placed in a tomb, a large stone is rolled in front of it and guards are placed at both sides of the entrance.

Mary's hope at life, her answer to every question, her ambassador of justice, her everything has been crucified and taken away, taking all sense of hope, experience, and light away. It's dark. Adhering to the strict laws of the Sabbath prohibiting activity, she has had to wait and now it is her first opportunity to muster up whatever inkling of strength she has left while still mourning, exhausted from the burden of bereavement, with hopes to anoint the body with oils and, in her estimation, give Jesus a proper burial.

While this account is presented in other Gospels, John is the only one who notes explicitly, "while it was still dark." I suggest that this darkness is beyond a time of day, but also a state of being, melancholy, devastation. It is not far-fetched to recognize that while it is perhaps dark for Mary physically, it is definitely dark emotionally. Yet refusing to be paralyzed by her pain, while it was still dark Mary stumbles to the tomb.

I think she sheds light on how we can handle dark moments in our lives. We are not strangers to dark moments. When you can be deemed dispensable because of the color of your skin, it is dark. When you can be discounted as inferior because of your gender, it's dark. When you are tossed aside like expired milk solely due to age, it's dark. When one person or group is so starving for power that they perpetuate the very systems that have isolated the other forever, under the umbrella of "there are good people on both sides," it's dark. When you can see someone trying to do well, and instead of celebrating them, we attempt to pull them down, it is dark.

The darkness does not absorb our responsibility, it requires it, it begs for it. We must go forward. Mary teaches us to, Just Go. Understanding that it is not always going to be the best situation, we still must go. It's not always going to be comfortable or convenient, but just like Mary, we are called to go forward. Go sit at the table of community leaders and help develop policies that benefit even the least of us. Go into systems to break cycles of poverty. Go and balance the scales between the haves and have-nots. The enemy would love nothing more than for you to be so frustrated and overwhelmed with life that you go backwards or sit and do nothing, but you must go forward. God has gone before you to make every crooked place straight, so go! He hasn't brought you this far to leave you now, go! Greater is He that is in you, go!

Mary goes and tells some of the other disciples, and then she too returns to the tomb. She doesn't seek anyone's approval. She doesn't waste time trying to prove that she is worthy of going. She just is. Similarly, I encourage you just to be. Just be who God has called you to be. Stop wasting precious Kingdom building time trying to prove who you are. When you walk in a room and the atmosphere shifts because you are there, it's clear. When you open your mouth and others are compelled to listen, your influence is evident. When what you lay your hands to works, it is clear. Just be!

In her dark experience, Mary returns to the tomb only to find that the body she was prepared to anoint is not there. Perhaps it was a flicker of hope that permeated her heart, allowing herself to have some closure through a proper burial and it's not even there. The flash of hope is instantly extinguished. It just got darker.

We've been there when you resolved to go forward in the dark, but then when you get to what you believe is the end, there is yet another issue to be dealt with. The situation suddenly gets darker. I know there are times in our lives and ministries when we just want to pull the cover over our heads and offer our own rendition of, "My God why has Thou forsaken me?"

The body is not there, and all she can fathom is that the body has been stolen, this is easier to wrap her troubled mind around, but she doesn't give up. She says to the man she thinks is the gardener, just tell me where He is, and I'll go get Him. She doesn't ask Him to do anything additional for her. She does what she can do. That's my final suggestion, just do what you can do. You and I must do what is in our power to do and trust God for the rest. We can't create a mountain, but we can speak to the mountain. We can't build a human, but we can love the humans God has placed around us. We can't add days to our lives, but we can bless God and live to the fullest the days He has given us! Do what you can do and trust God for the rest!

This sister is broken but not backing down, in the dark but still determined. It's dark, but she refuses to give up, she refuses to go back. We too must refuse to give up, refuse to turn back, or backpedal the road to justice and success. The God we serve has been too good and done too much! There is much at stake, so go forward. You have what you need. You can get it done without becoming undone.

Check List:

1. How will you move forward into your purpose?
2. When dark moments come, what will push you through?
3. What's at stake if you move forward? What's at stake if you don't?

The Get It Done Declaration

I will accomplish the tasks set before me and still have joy on the journey. I will not become undone.

I will prioritize purposefully. I will not try to burn the candle at both ends.

I will be Spirit-led, purpose-filled, and intentional in my planning. I will not get swept into the world of thinking that busyness is success.

I will push even when I don't feel like it. I will not be run by emotions.

I will take and plan breaks before they are necessary. I will not feel guilty about resting.

I will trust that God has given me everything that I need to be successful. I will not be overwhelmed or overtaken.

I will follow through and finish strong on God-given tasks. I will not stop short of success.

I will maintain integrity as I succeed and fulfill my God-given potential. I will not let others define what success is to me.

I will be fueled by the Spirit of God. I will not expect everyone to like, understand, appreciate, or celebrate my passions and practices.

I will be intentional about taking care of me so that I can better care for others. I don't want to pour from an empty place.

I will celebrate my strengths. I will not beat myself up over mistakes.

I will not compare myself to others' purposes or paths. I will run my schedule not let my schedule run me.

I will surround myself by others who are on a quest to fulfill their God-given purpose.

By the grace of God, I will get it done!

About the Author

Rev. Dr. Jennell Whitfield Riddick

As a wife, mother, speaker, author, community leader, and non-profit founder, Rev. Dr. Jennell Whitfield Riddick's undeniable passion and sincere desire to encourage, empower, and equip others to "walk in" their maximum potential fuels her daily. Honored by the privilege to share with thousands over a decade, it is evident that improving the lives of others is her life's work.

Dr. Jennell Whitfield Riddick is an honors graduate of the University of Richmond where she double majored in Rhetoric and Communication Studies and Theatre. She served in numerous leadership capacities and as a part of several organizations. She is also an honors graduate of the Samuel DeWitt Proctor School of Theology at Virginia Union University where she earned a Master of Divinity Degree. She received her Doctoral Degree from Chicago Theological Seminary.

Mrs. Riddick is the recipient of the National Black Student Leadership Conference Legacy Award, the Rhetoric and Communication Studies Leadership Award, the Westhampton College Distinguished Leadership Award, the University Players Best Lead Actress Award, and the Peer Advisory and Mentor Program Mentor of the Year. She was named the Community Service Woman of the Year among many other awards.

Dr. Riddick is the Founder and Executive Director of Walk in It Inc. This organization is devoted to the holistic health and empowerment of girls and women. Walk In It's Ladies of Distinction Mentor/Character Development Program officially launched in the 2007–2008 school year with approximately 16 high school ladies in a single school. Since its inception, the program has experienced exponential growth. At the time of printing, Ladies of Distinction Program currently serves over 650 girls monthly throughout 23 schools in 5 school districts. (Suffolk, Chesapeake, Southampton, Franklin, and Hampton). Through the implementation of this program, schools have reported tremendous improvement in grades and overall behavior.

Additionally, Walk In It has awarded thousands of dollars in scholarships. Observing a need to equip students with skills and information to engage in healthy relationships with peers, adults, and in dating relationships, Riddick has hosted 12 Healthy Relationship Conferences. Recognizing the connection between positive self-esteem and self-efficacy, Walk In It has organized eight Self-Esteem Empowerment Walks and Rallies, bringing together hundreds of girls and women annually.

Adult women are also empowered through annual women's conferences and the R.E.D. (Raising Excellent Daughters) Program which addresses the needs of parents. Dr. Riddick is also part of multiple community initiatives.

Mrs. Riddick is employed as the Director of Ministries at First Baptist Church in Franklin, VA. She also serves as an Adjunct Instructor at Paul D. Camp Community College. Jennell Riddick is the author of *Walk In It: Advancing*

Beyond Average, and *Girl Talk: What Every Lady Should Know*. She continues to travel as a highly sought-after motivational speaker, conference facilitator, minister, and mentor.

For more information about Dr. Jennell Riddick or to request her to speak at one of your upcoming events, please visit:

www.walkinit.com

www.witlod.org

or Email: admin@walkinit.com

www.ingramcontent.com/pod-product-compliance
Lightning Source LLC
Chambersburg PA
CBHW052114070526
44584CB00017B/2483